Table of Contents

Home and

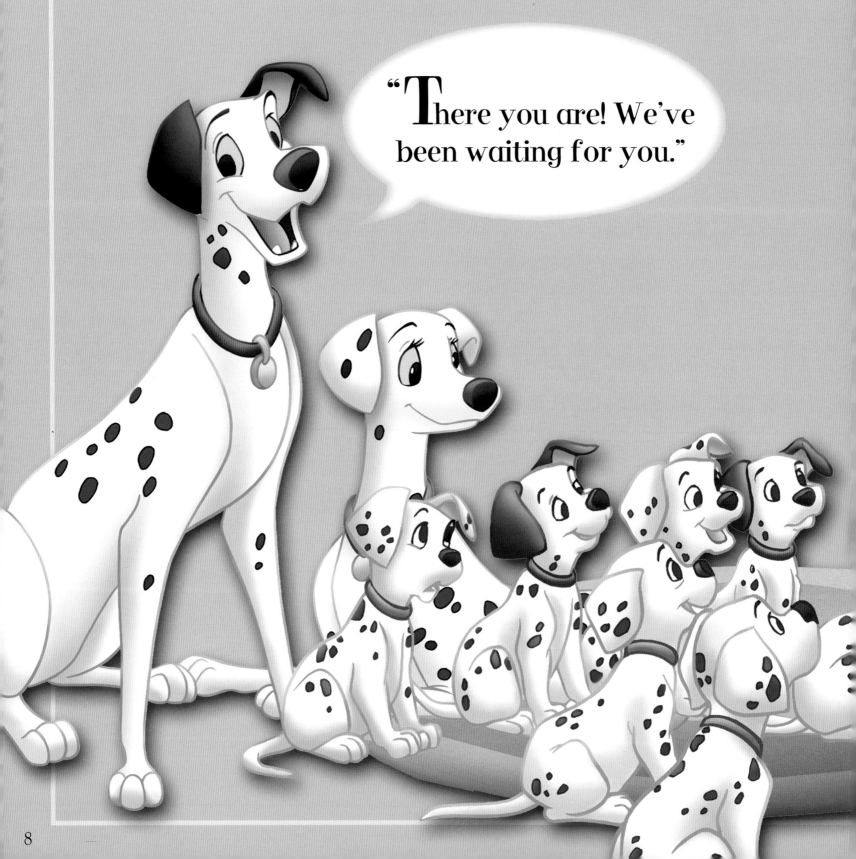

"There you are! We've been waiting for you."

Family

Turn the page to see what's going

on at Mickey's . Find out who meets

a new . Discover all the things growing

in 🦆's garden. Help 🐻 tuck 👧 in.

And, 👧 needs your help in the kitchen.

But beware! Look who loses

his temper when you find him

in the .

All Kinds of Families!

How many family members do you have?

father
mother
brother
sister
brother

the Darling family

daughters
father
daughters

Ariel's family

queen
king
princess

Sleeping Beauty's family

husband

granddaughter

wife

pets

the Dalmatians' family

mother   father

grandmother

Mulan's family

uncle

nephews

Donald's family

mother

child

Dumbo's family

11

Mickey's House

clothes

lawnmower

kennel

window

"I'm glad you came to visit me!"

garden

chimney

roof

porch

fence

house

nails

front door

saw

drive

toolbox

hammer

garage door

car

letter box

garage

washing line

wood

birdbox

13

Daisy's Garden

wheelbarrow

seeds

plants

worm

vine

water

soil

rake

cane

watering can

sprinkler

seed packet

hedge

CAN YOU FIND?

five snails

trowel

hose pipe

sunflower

15

The 101 Dalmatians' Living Room

fireplace

armchair

television

floor

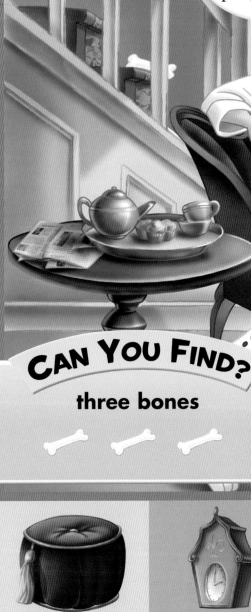

"It's time for our favourite programme!"

CAN YOU FIND?

three bones

wallpaper

footstool

clock

lamp

light switch

banister

rug

vacuum
cleaner

settee

bookcase

books

radiator

vase

coffee table

lampshade

staircase

17

Lilo's and Nani's Kitchen

measuring jug

mop

saucepan

refrigerator

dishwasher

"Help me stop all these bubbles!"

frying pan

rolling pin

sponge

kettle

sink

18

blender

cupboard

soap suds

oven

ironing board

tea towel

tap

kitchen towel

iron

rubbish bin

CAN YOU FIND?

three mugs

toaster

cooker

apron

dustpan

brush

19

Beauty and the Beast's Dining Room

cup

dish

knife

plate

"Be our guest! Dinner is served!"

table

spoon

jug

fork

saucer

china cupboard

napkin

chandelier

sugar bowl

teapot

glass

CAN YOU FIND?

a salt pot and
a pepper pot

candlestick

tongs

place mat

milk jug

ladle

bowl

21

Dinner for Two for Lady and the Tramp!

spaghetti and meatballs

pizza

rice

pasta

soup

sausage

toast

baguette

crackers

ham

jam

prawn

cheese

milk

roast beef

butter

eggs

tuna

sandwich

lobster

bacon

peanut butter

steak

yoghurt

salt

pepper

hamburger

cereal

chicken

ketchup

"Which are *your* favourite foods?"

chips

tea

Snow White's Apple and a Feast of Fruits

apple

banana

cherries

pear

melons

strawberries

raspberries

blueberries

blackberries

watermelons

mango

avocados

papayas

pineapple

peach

plums

raisins

coconuts

oranges

grapefruit

grapes

lemons

limes

"Take a bite, my dear."

A Pumpkin Takes Cinderella to the Ball!

garlic

courgettes

aubergine

lettuce

gherkins

beetroot

"Be home by midnight, before the coach turns into a pumpkin!"

olives

 cauliflower

 spinach

 Brussels sprouts

 radishes

 celery

 peppers

 broccoli

 tomato

 cucumber

 potatoes

 French beans

 beans

 onion

 pumpkin

 cabbage

 carrots

 sweetcorn

 peas

 mushrooms

27

Donald's Bathroom

bathrobe

medicine cupboard

soap

hairdryer

"You're in my bathroom!"

hairbrush

comb

toilet paper

towel rail

bubbles

bath towel

shampoo

shower cap

flannel

shower

toilet

toothbrush

mirror

CAN YOU FIND?
three rubber ducks

yacht

toothpaste

nailbrush

bath

Babysitting in the Nursery

pram

mobile

bib

rocking chair

"Look . . . it's a baby!"

bottle

nappy

teething ring

dummy

with Lady and the Tramp

baby

cradle

bonnet

curtains

CAN YOU FIND?

one rattle

high chair

cot

talcum powder

teddy bear

Who's in Boo's Bedroom?

bedside table

pillow

picture

bed

telephone

carpet

sheet

bedspread

shelf

 alarm clock

dressing gown

 chest of drawers

 toy box

 blanket

"Shh ! Sweet dreams, Boo!"

CAN YOU FIND?

two slippers

 pillowcase

 box

 drawer

hanger

 door

33

Cinderella Dresses the Mice

tiara

hat

gloves

boots

suit

ballet shoes

coat

umbrella

jumper

skirt

high heels

gown

raincoat

sandals

hair bow

cap

belt

scarf

shirt

bow tie

socks

T-shirt

tutu

blouse

shoes

dungarees

tie

jacket

shorts

handbag

snowshoes

trainers

trousers

tuxedo

"Cinderellie, you have great taste in clothes!"

jeans

cloak

dress

mittens

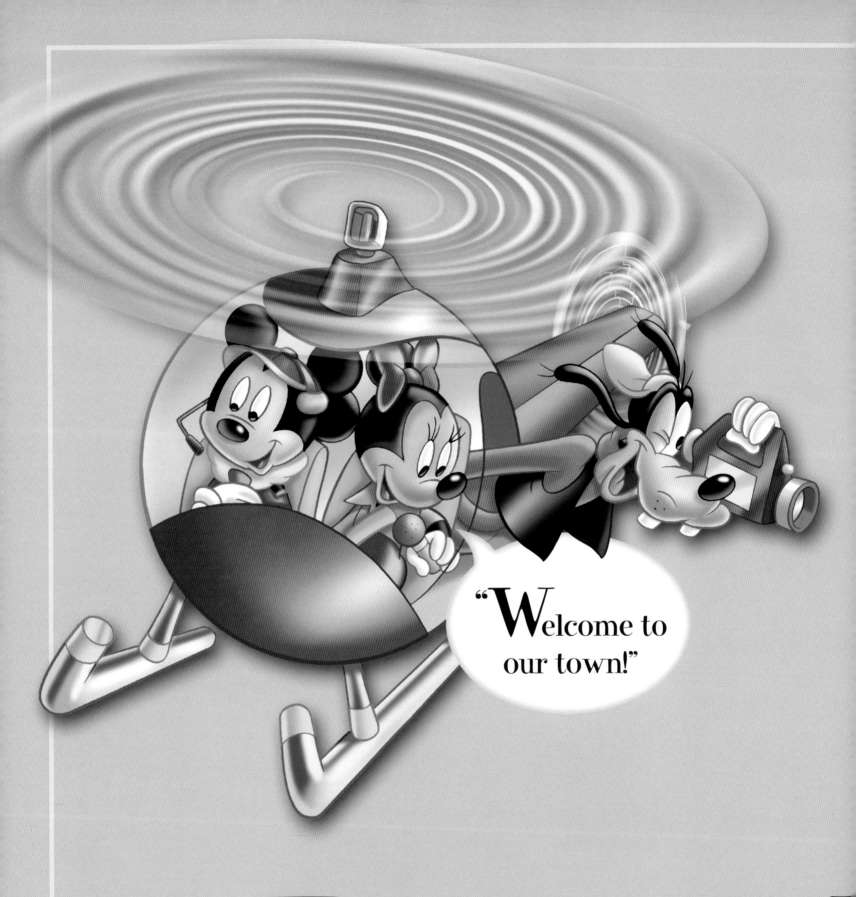

Town and

There's so much to do and see. What would

you like to do first? Would you like to see

or a ? Do you want to join and

 as they post a letter at the post office?

Would you like to ride a or catch a

 to visit Andy in his classroom? It

might be fun to talk to a or a

and learn what they do. Why not end

your adventure with and an ?

Community

Mickey and Friends Tour the Town

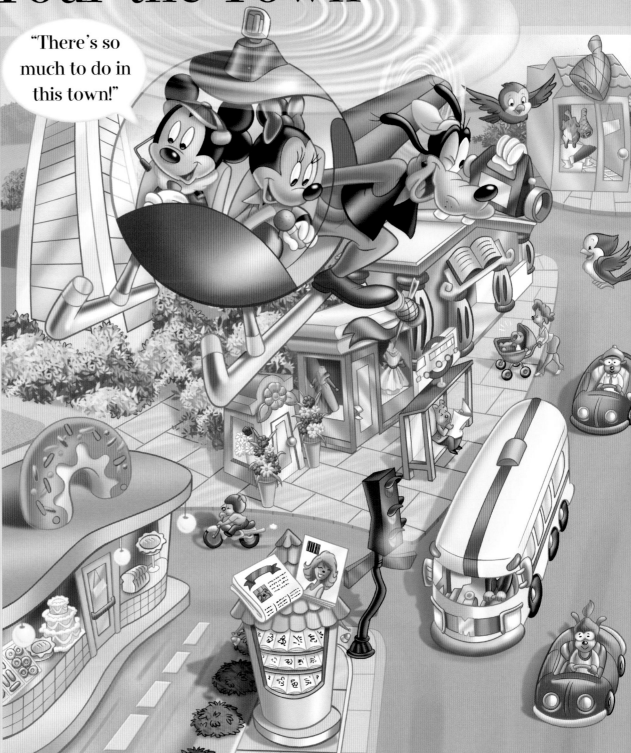

"There's so much to do in this town!"

bakery

bank

bus stop

florist

dress shop

awning

magazine

sweet shop

newsagent

lamp-post

road

department store

cinema

office building

apartment building

butcher

restaurant

newspaper

library

grocery

traffic light

39

Buzz Lightyear in the Toy Shop

electric train

dinosaur

action figure

piggy bank

soft toys

board game

jigsaw

chess

spinning top

bricks

doll

rocking horse

toys

spaceship

space ranger

dominoes

playing cards

telescope

draughts

41

Minnie at the Department Store

"What should I buy?"

VCR

necklaces

screwdriver

drill

pliers

CD player

mouse mat

silver ring

mobile phone

bracelets

printer

radio

watch

calculator

computer mouse

earrings

gold ring

£1

CAN YOU FIND?

two nails

video camera

camera

wrench

tape recorder

jewels

computer

Mike and Celia in the Restaurant

cashier

chopsticks

ice

soy sauce

booth

iced tea

money

menu

44

jukebox

credit card

"Only the best for Schmoopsie... and you, too!"

waiter

counter

till

CAN YOU FIND?
four small fish

coins

wallet

sushi

bill

sushi chef

45

101 Dalmatians at the Sweetshop

"Mmm! I love ice cream . . . don't you?"

CAN YOU FIND?

three cherries

maple syrup

muffins

doughnuts

biscuits

hundreds and thousands

croissants

cupcakes

ice cream

shortbread

ice-cream sundae

chopped nuts

hot chocolate

milkshake

whipped cream

sweets

crumpets

waffle

ice-cream cone

pie

fruit punch

Lilo and Stitch at the Post Office

postage stamps

ink pad

notice board

clerk

"It's fun at the post office!"

address book

rubber stamp

envelope

postbag

parcel

queue

address

postman

letter

poster

CAN YOU FIND?
four balls of string

keys

post

map pins

postcard

scissors

Buzz and Woody at Andy's School

"Tell Andy we're outside!"

teacher

graph paper

chalk

blackboard

comic

pencil

coat hooks

map

glasses

desk

schoolbag

textbook

lunch box

notebook

felt-tip pens

globe

CAN YOU FIND?

three apples

glue

pens

rubber

wax crayon

ruler

Lady and the Tramp at the Vet's

"We're here for a check-up!"

ubber gloves

 vet

 waiting room

 cotton-wool balls

examining table

 lab coat

 bandage

 stethoscope

syringe

dog collar

 mask

 thermometer

scales

tissues

 lead

dog tag

 X-ray

 microscope

 filing cabinet

 file

CAN YOU FIND?

four cotton-wool buds

Donald Visits the Fire Station

fire station

chief fire officer

axe

firefighter

"Are you laughing at me, too? That makes me so cross!"

water hose

wheel

54

fire engine

fire hydrant

steering wheel

ladder

bell

fire extinguisher

CAN YOU FIND?

three pairs of boots

helmet

pole

braces

loudspeaker

hubcap

alarm

Aladdin Takes a Ride

rowing boat

tricycle

tugboat

mobile home

double-decker bus

ferry

ambulance

houseboat

taxi

boat

bicycle

lorry

removal van

submarine

tanker

motorcycle

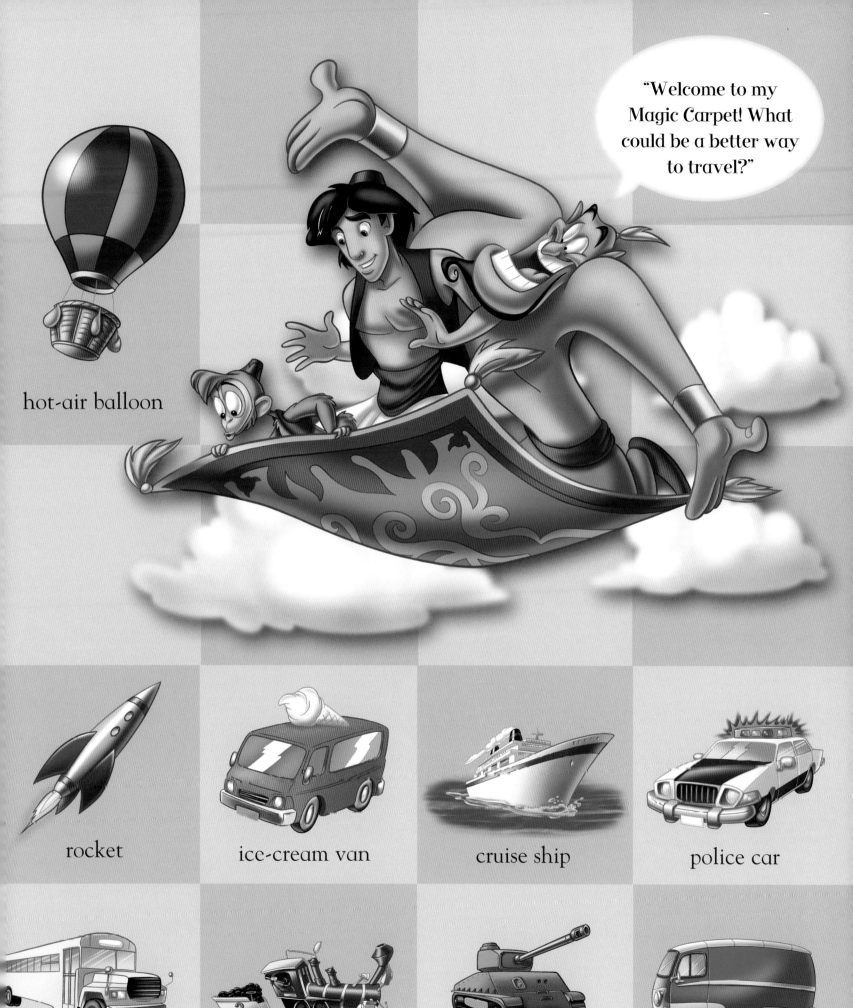

hot-air balloon

"Welcome to my Magic Carpet! What could be a better way to travel?"

rocket

ice-cream van

cruise ship

police car

school bus

train

tank

van

57

Buzz Finds a Toy Bulldozer

dumper truck

cement mixer

forklift truck

crane

bulldozer

tractor

snowplough

58

plough

road sweeper

breakdown lorry

pick-up truck

dustbin lorry

steamroller

Mickey and Friends at the Airport

jet plane

customs

wing

flight attendant

engine

propeller

fuel tanker

pilot

suitcase

aeroplane

passport

passenger

customs officer

control tower

ticket agent

"Wow! Look at all these passengers!"

check-in desk

lounge

luggage label

tail

61

Monsters at Work

athlete

doctor

carpenter

police officer

magician

TV presenter

ballet dancer

sailor

librarian

photographer

chef

builder

bus driver

62

hairdresser

painter

cleaner

plumber

astronaut

secretary

nurse

doorman

dentist

car mechanic

grocer

taxi driver

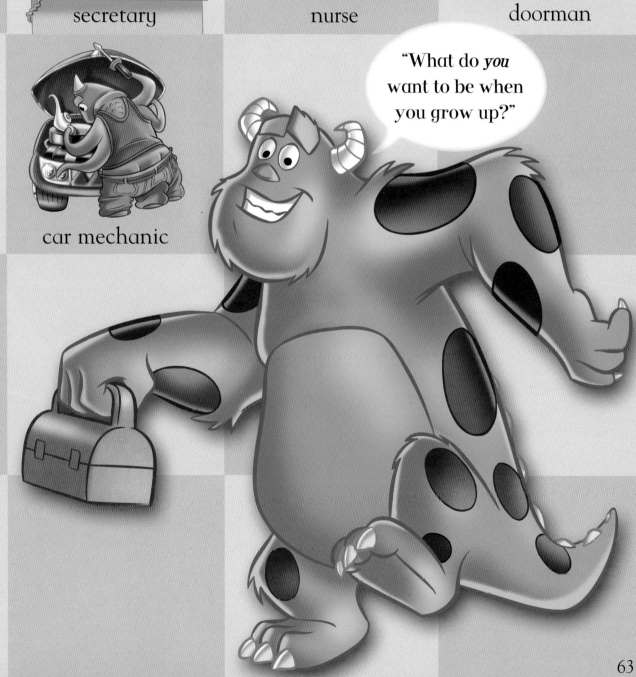

"What do *you* want to be when you grow up?"

Having Fun

"Hey, there! Are you ready to have some fun?"

Just turn the page and join at the circus. Throw a to . Dance with . Pose for a picture with . Go to the amusement park with and taste some . Then play on the beach, building a with . Have a great time!

Dumbo at the Circus

cage

big top

sword

CAN YOU FIND?

six peanuts

clown

top hat

ringmaster

megaphone

juggler

tails

feather

trapeze artist

tight
rope

hoop

trapeze

lion
tamer

net

Pongo and Perdita at the Amusement Park

fun house

fudge

haunted house

dragon

"Wow, we can see everything from the big wheel!"

drawbridge

ticket

tower

ticket collector

monkey

candy floss

organ grinder

big wheel

roller coaster

moat

ghosts

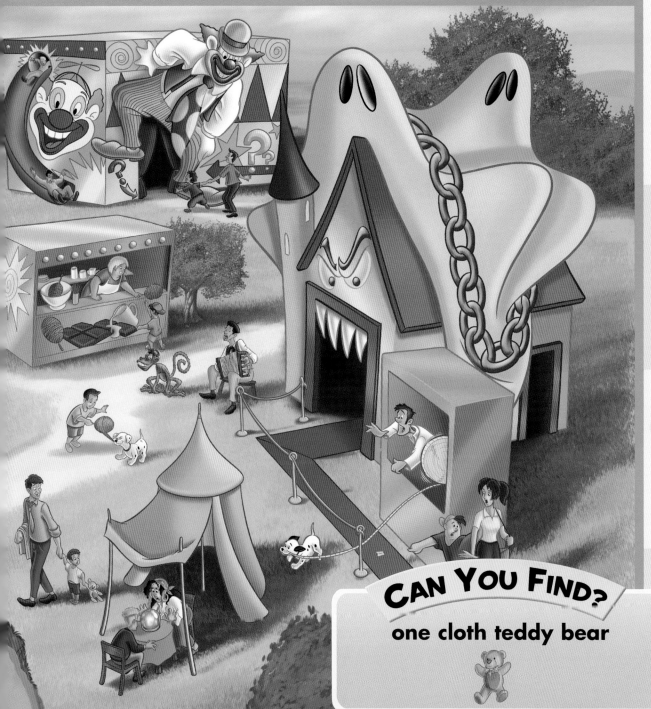

CAN YOU FIND?
one cloth teddy bear

castle

carousel

crystal ball

fortune teller

pedalo

Playing in the Park with Lady and the Tramp

jogger

park

fountain

statue

kite

wind

birdbath

flag

bench

pigeon

path

merry-go-round

flagpole

litter bin

CAN YOU FIND?

Si and Am

string

71

At the Playground with Mickey

slide

skipping rope

see-saw

swings

handle

rollerblades

hopscotch

spade

quoits

sandpit

"Our uncle Mickey is the greatest!"

bar

tag

bucket

CAN YOU FIND?

two balls

skateboard

marbles

climbing frame

water fountain

73

Donald's Day of Sports

swimming

ice hockey

basketball

"Hey! Watch that ball!"

ice-skating

football

American football

tennis

 hockey

 polo

 archery

 table tennis

 rowing

 cycling

 cricket

 jogging

 snowboarding

 weightlifting

 skiing

75

Miss Bianca Paints a Picture

palette

paper

artist

canvas

painting

rag

sketches

paintbrush

portrait

clay

ceramics

pottery

kiln

potter's wheel

paint

smock

easel

"I'd love to paint your portrait!"

77

The Aristocats
Move to the Music

piano

sheet music

trumpet

musical notes

piano keys

flute

pedal

double bass

drumsticks

saxophone

mouth organ

trombone

metronome

78

music
stand

guitar

drums

violin

bow

musician

drummer

singer

baton

tuba

clarinet

piccolo

cymbals

tambourine

bugle

oboe

xylophone

bass drum

French horn

accordion

marching band

dancers

parade

confetti

81

Lilo and Stitch on the Beach

swimming trunks

beach ball

surfboard

CAN YOU FIND?

two starfish

beach towel

sunglasses

sun hat

beach

waves

swimming costume

sun cream

seaweed

lifeguard

sea

deckchair

parasol

"Surf's up! Come on in!"

sand

seagull

shell

sandcastle

life jacket

83

Monsters, Inc., at the Cinema

84

screen

row

film

paper cup

popcorn

aisle

torch

film reel

projector

usher

seat

straw

actors

drink

CAN YOU FIND?

four cinema tickets

A *Toy Story* Birthday Party

candles

paper plates

party hat

streamers

birthday cake

rattle

party blower

balloons

presents

wrapping paper

ribbon

birthday card

CAN YOU FIND?

three pink ribbons

A Beauty and the Beast Christmas

tinsel

ornaments

snowballs

wreath

icicle

sledge

garland

angel

HAVING FUN

"Don't you just love holidays!"

Christmas tree

muff

snowman

sleigh bells

CAN YOU FIND?

eight pine cones

snowflake

sleigh

popcorn chain

Animals

"Hello! Welcome to the great outdoors!"

and Nature

Just turn the pages to meet a , a , an and so much more!

You can go hiking with Robin Hood. Go for a walk in the forest and see . Pick a or smell a . Discover all the amazing animals under the sea with .

Lilo Goes to the Pet Shop

CAN YOU FIND?

three pet collars

"Will you help me choose the best pet?"

cat food

guinea pig

cat

puppies

turtle

rabbits

birdcage

goldfish

canary

fishbowl

aquarium

hamsters

dog

ferret

snake

iguana

kittens

93

ANIMALS AND NATURE

101 Dalmatians Visit the Farm

weather vane

farmhouse

scarecrow

turkey

"Oh, no! The puppies have got out!"

duckling

goose

cow

goat

barn

piglet

chicks

cockerel

hens

lamb

foal

kids

henhouse

donkey

hay

horse

calf

pig

sheep

95

On the Plain with Simba

gazelle

lion cub

gorilla

lion

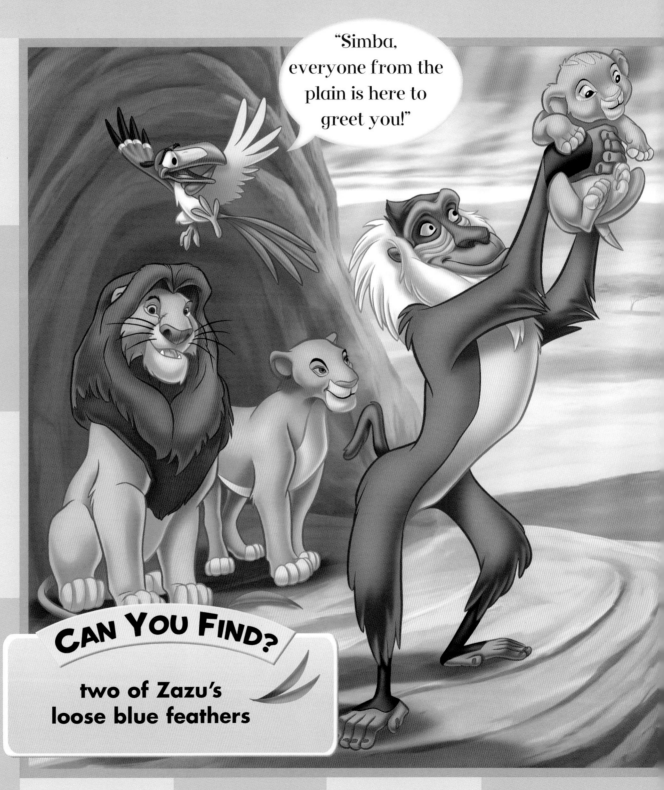

"Simba, everyone from the plain is here to greet you!"

CAN YOU FIND?

two of Zazu's loose blue feathers

rhino

chimpanzee

cheetah

hornbill

zebra

giraffe

baboon

wildebeest

elephant

hippo

leopard

hyena

lioness

Lilo's Book of Wild Animals

crocodile

python

vulture

jaguar

poison-arrow frog

coyote

tarantula

grizzly bear

king cobra

tiger

Gila monster

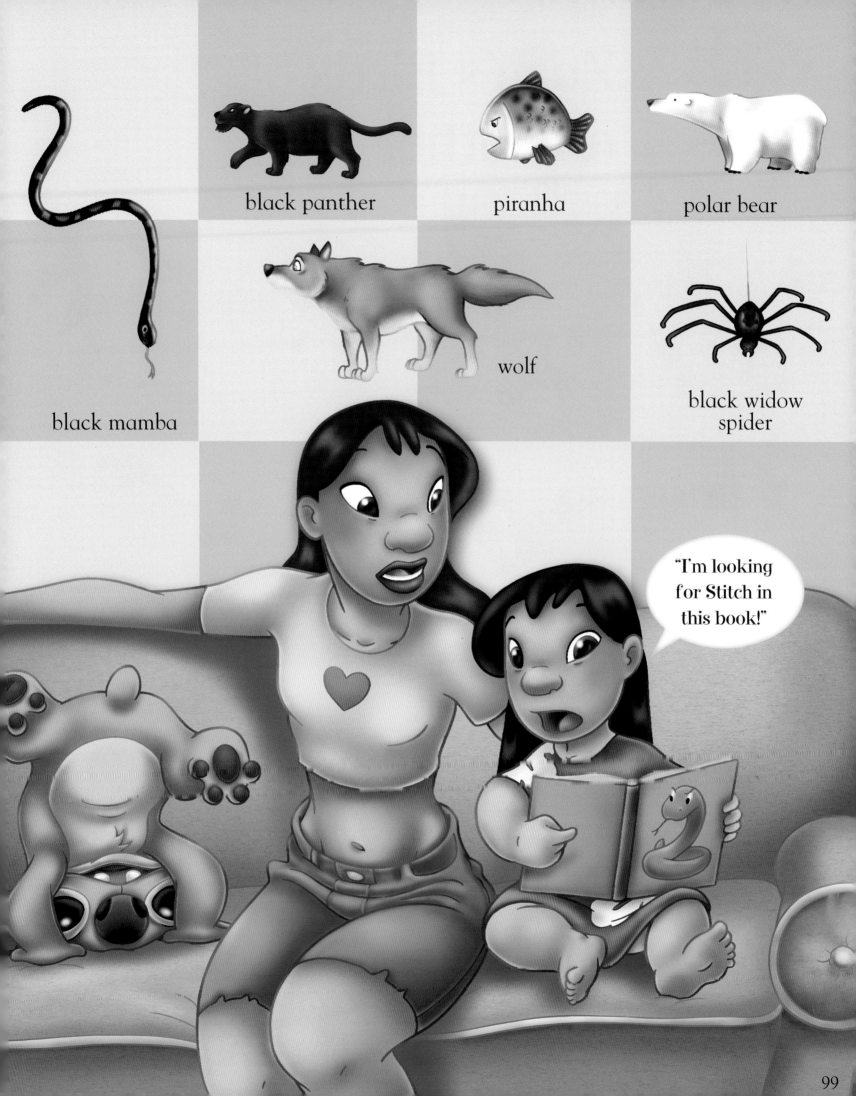

black mamba

black panther

piranha

polar bear

wolf

black widow
spider

"I'm looking for Stitch in this book!"

Zazu's Birds of a Feather

flamingo

hawk

blue jay

penguin

robin

bald eagle

toucan

hummingbird

magpie

swan

budgerigar

parrot

dove

bluebird

kingfisher

crow

pelican

puffin

stork

macaw

"Please! Help Simba find some other birds!"

ostrich

101

Bambi's Forest Friends

CAN YOU FIND?

five acorns

opossums

otter

moose

doe

butterfly

raccoon

fawn

porcupine

102

beaver

chipmunk

bird's nest

skunk

spider

spider's web

badger

owl

stag

fox

frog

squirrel

woodpecker

103

Goofy's Photo Safari

"L-l-look! I photographed these animals all by myself!"

giant panda

manatee

armadillo

orang-utan

hedgehog

manatee

104

walrus

chameleon

kangaroo

sloth

reindeer

anteater

camel

snail

koala bear

Ariel Plays in the Sea

seal

flounder

coral

clown fish

crab

shark

jellyfish

starfish

dolphin

merman

octopus

eel

whale

mermaid

squid

sea horse

minnow

sea turtle

Flik Finds the Circus Bugs

bumblebee

grasshopper

cricket

rhinoceros beetle

ladybird

caterpillar

moth

stick insect

woodlouse

dragonfly

horsefly

ant

wasp

firefly

praying mantis

flea

daddy longlegs

greenfly

hornet

Robin Hood's Mountain Trail Adventure

stream

track

water bottle

rainbow

branch

cloud

roots

sky

tree

110

waterfall

mountain

cave

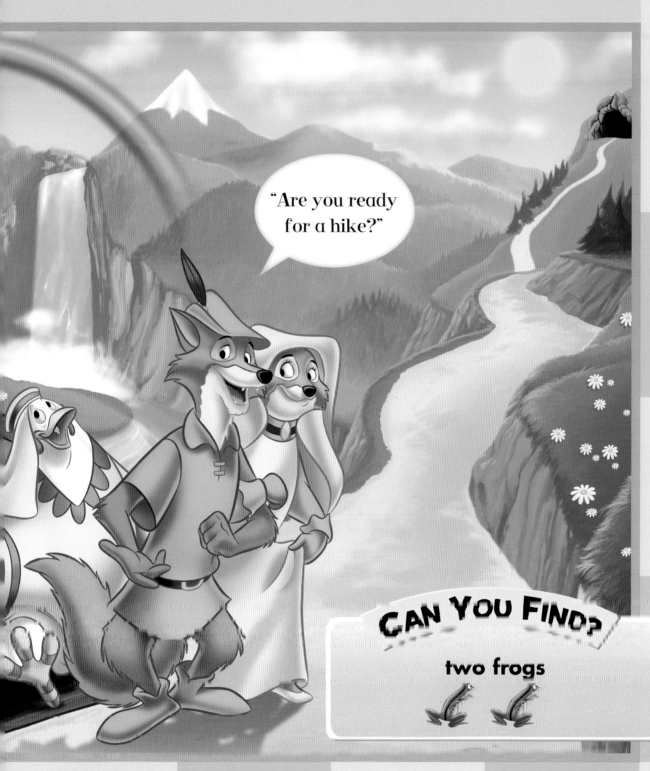

"Are you ready for a hike?"

CAN YOU FIND?

two frogs

bridge

bark

sun

leaf

hole

shadow

Flower's Lovely Flowers

daisy

rose

lilac

tiger lily

dahlia

bluebell

carnation

tulip

baby's breath

112

orchid

poppies

violet

daffodil

wild flowers

pussy willow

"You can call me Flower if you want to!"

Peter Pan's Camping Trip

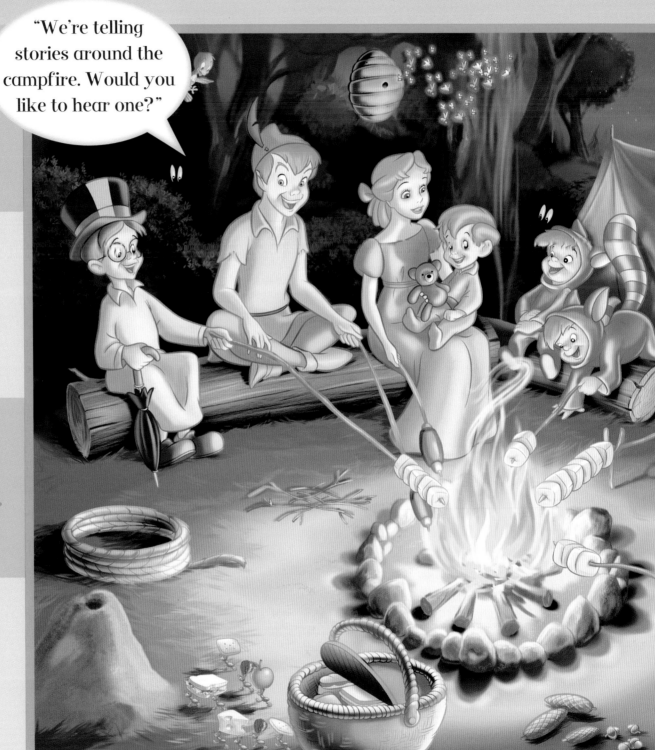

"We're telling stories around the campfire. Would you like to hear one?"

campfire

marshmallows

hot dogs

sleeping bag

picnic basket

log

smoke

rocks

twigs

rope

tent

beehive

grass

bushes

fishing rod

acorns

pine cones

anthill

CAN YOU FIND?

two pairs of yellow eyes hidden in the bushes

forest

moon

stars

bats

lantern

Things to

"It's nice to meet you! I'm a real boy now!"

Know

I can ![dance]. In winter I get ![cold] and just like you, I get ![messy]! Turn the pages to see colours like ![leaf] and ![leaf]. Or use your ![Pinocchio] to count numbers like ![one dog] and ![two dogs]. Can you find shapes like a ![heart] and a ![circle]? Whatever you do, just be happy!

Pinocchio Becomes a Real Boy

head

toes

ear

cheek

eyelashes

eyes

nose

chin

neck

wrist

fingernails

waist

thigh

leg

ankle

feet

hip

 shoulder

 hair

hands

 arm

 teeth

eyebrows

 knee

tongue

fingers

elbow

 mouth

119

All Kinds of Feelings

sleepy

proud

silly

guilty

grumpy

sad

hungry

angry

scared

"Good morning, Snow White! You look cheerful today!"

Four Seasons with Bambi

spring rain

"The rain tastes so sweet!"

summer sunshine

"The flowers smell so good!"

123

THINGS TO KNOW

A Busy Year for Princesses

JANUARY

FEBRUARY

MAY

JUNE

SEPTEMBER

OCTOBER

MARCH

APRIL

JULY

AUGUST

NOVEMBER

DECEMBER

Monday

Tuesday

Wednesday

Thursday

Friday

Saturday

Sunday

How Many Dalmatians?

1 one

2 two

3 three

4 four

5 five

6 six

7 seven

8 eight

9 nine

10 ten

"How many puppies are there?"

11 eleven

12 twelve

13 thirteen

14 fourteen

15 fifteen

16 sixteen

17 seventeen

18 eighteen

19 nineteen

20 twenty

127

Finding Shapes in Wonderland

CAN YOU FIND?

four teacups

"How very curious things are here!"

THIS WAY

rectangle

triangle

star

crescent

heart

diamond

oval

cone

cube

square

circle

129

Pocahontas Sees Lots of Colours

white

red

pink

orange

yellow

purple

blue

grey

brown

green

black

CAN YOU FIND?

two sacks

131

Aladdin's Favourite Opposites

big

small

"I'll catch you, you sneaky little monkey!"

bad

good

slow

fast

cold   hot

dry   wet

open   closed

fat   thin

quiet   noisy

new   old

Busy Beauty, Busy Beast!

sing

clean

jump

stand

eat

"What things do *you* like to do?"

smile

talk

read

whisper

listen

think

laugh

write

sleep

sit

build

wake up

drink

kiss

run

dance

135

Hide-and-Seek with Simba and Nala

far/near

"I am left and Nala is right!"

left/right

below/above

through

in front of/behind

around

under/over

on/off

out/in

INDEX

139

141

Dalmatian

Goofy

Mike

Dumbo

Mrs Potts and Chip

Sulley

Pinocchio

Cinderella

Snow White

Tinker Bell

Mickey

Woody

Stitch

Timon

Mowgli

Aladdin